A Little

Herb

Cookbook

Maril·
Illustrated by

Apple

First published in 1995 by
The Appletree Press Ltd
19–21 Alfred Street, Belfast BT2 8DL
Tel. +44 (0) 1232 243074
Fax +44 (0) 1232 246756
Copyright © 1995 The Appletree Press, Ltd.

A Little Herb Cookbook

A catalogue record for this book is available
in The British Library.

ISBN 0-86281-532-0

9 8 7 6 5 4 3 2

Introduction

History does not relate the identity of the person who first discovered the bliss of a tomato eaten with fresh basil, or thought to marry sage with onion in a stuffing, or lamb with rosemary and garlic. We do know that most of the flavour-enhancing herbs we enjoy today were prized by the earliest cultures to relieve diets that were often dull and limited.

Culinary and medicinal herbs were cherished through the middle ages in monastery gardens and great estates as well as humble cottages, only to go into decline as the industrial revolution effected mass production of food.

Happily, new generations are turning back to natural foods and seasonings that please the palate while they delight the eye. Herbs, with their graceful looks and delicious scents, are being rediscovered for recipes that are as old as the Hanging Gardens and as modern as this morning's inspiration.

A note on measures
Metric, imperial and volume measurements are given for all recipes. For best results, use one set only. The strength of herbs may vary according to their cultivars, growing conditions and storage, so make adjustments according to your own taste. Recipes are for 4 unless otherwise indicated.

A Bouquet of Herbs

Fresh herbs are silver and gold for the cook, whether they are grown in a beautiful walled garden, a corner of the vegetable patch or in the window box of a city dweller. The posy of herbs listed below has a place in every kitchen.

Basil Sweet basil and the smaller-leaved bush basil are the most common forms of this spicy, scented summer herb. Used fresh, the leaves of this sun-loving herb have a clove-like aroma that marries especially well with tomatoes, pasta and egg dishes. Basil loses its unique flavour when dried.

Bay Useful throughout the year, wreaths of this noble laurel once crowned ancient heroes. Most aromatic when dried, bay leaves are a vital part of the classic *bouquet garni* and useful for soups, stews and casseroles as well as marinades for meat, fish and game.

Chives This grass-like member of the onion family grows obligingly outdoors or in window-sill pots, flourishing with regular clipping. The mild onion-flavoured leaves are used fresh in salads as well as in cheese, egg and vegetable dishes, when they should be added toward the end of cooking. Freeze-dried chives are best when fresh are not available.

Coriander Both leaves and seeds of this warmly pungent herb are valuable in the kitchen. Green leaves resemble flat-leafed parsley and are much favoured in Indian, Mexican and Middle Eastern dishes. Use freshly chopped in salads and *salsas*, or add at the last moment to hot dishes and soups.

parsley

bay leaves

coriander

chives

tarragon

marjoram

mint

rosemary

sage

Dill Much prized in Scandinavia and cooler climes, this feathery herb with its distinctive flavour is popularly associated with fresh salmon, potato salad and pickled cucumbers. It has a natural affinity with seafood of all sorts, cream cheese and green beans.

Fennel Feathery fronds of fennel may look like dill, but are distinguished by a definite aniseed taste. This is the classic fish herb, useful for stuffings, sauces and as a bed for grilled seafood.

Garlic Pungently aromatic, this controversial bulb of the onion family is one of the oldest culinary herbs. From China to Mexico, many ethnic cuisines feature garlic as an essential flavouring. Strongest in its raw state, garlic takes on a sweeter, milder character in cooking and enhances the flavour of other ingredients. It is used in soups, sauces, stews and virtually every type of savoury dish.

Marjoram The small leaves of this mildly spicy plant can be used fresh in summer and dried in winter. Often described as a meat herb, it also complements fish, cheese, tomato and egg dishes. Wild marjoram has a stronger flavour and is generally known by its Italian name of oregano, an essential seasoning for pizza and many Mediterranean specialities.

Mint There are numerous varieties of this fresh-scented herb, from applemint to eau-de-cologne and lemon mint, all most strongly flavoured when grown in full sun. Used for refreshing teas, drinks and sweets, it is rarely used in the West for savouries, while Eastern foods often combine mint and spices in chicken and meat specialities.

Parsley Vitamin-rich fresh parsley is available year round and should only be used dried as a last resort. The fresh colour and taste of its leaves enhance salads and every sort of savoury food, while stems contain most flavour for soups and stocks. Flat-leafed or continental parsley is the variety preferred for culinary use.

Rosemary Needle-like leaves of rosemary are strongly pungent and best used cautiously to complement lamb, poultry and game. It also goes well with potatoes, beans, and tomato-based sauces. Rosemary is best dried in summer when its aromatic oils are strongest.

Sage The classic herb for stuffings, sage counteracts the fattiness of duck, goose and pork. It is essential in many types of sausage and also enhances tomato and cheese-based dishes. Unlike many herbs, it has a stronger flavour when dried and must be used cautiously.

Tarragon The delicate aniseed flavour of tarragon highlights classic *bearnaise* sauce, sophisticated salad dressings and elegant chicken and egg dishes. Long cooking decreases the strength of tarragon and it is generally added to dishes near the end of cooking.

Thyme There are scores of thyme varieties, all delightfully aromatic and useful in long-cooked dishes like stews and soups. Thyme is a vital element of the classical *bouquet garni* and dries well, although it is strongest when used fresh.

Preserving and Storing Herbs

Late summer is usually the best time to save herbs, when their aromatic oils are at a peak. Bay, marjoram, mint, rosemary, sage, tarragon and thyme dry well if hung in small bunches in a warm airy

place away from direct sunlight. As soon as the leaves are dry and brittle, they should be stripped from the stems and stored in airtight containers away from light and heat.

Basil, chives, dill, fennel and parsley lose much of their character when dried, but can be successfully frozen. Chop the fresh herbs and freeze in a little water in ice cube trays. Chopped parsley can simply be frozen in polythene bags ready for use. Many cooks feel that the seeds of fennel and dill give better flavour in winter than any attempt at preserving summer greenery.

Flavourful herbs like basil, thyme, tarragon and rosemary can be infused in bottles of oil or vinegar to be used in salad dressings and marinades when fresh herbs are not available.

Herbs in Classic Combinations

Bouquet Garni This culinary term refers to a posy of parsley, a thyme sprig and leaf or two of bay tied together and used to flavour slowly cooked soups, braises and stews. Fresh or dried herbs can be used and they are sometimes tied into the hollow of a celery stalk.

Fines Herbes Traditional French cooks' mixture of 4 freshly chopped or dried herbs – parsley, chervil, chives and tarragon. This is used for sprinkling over fresh salads or in egg, chicken and fish dishes, added at the end of cooking.

Herbes de Provence Originally a regional mixture of sun-loving herbs from Mediterranean hills, *herbes de Provence* is now a universally popular seasoning. Thyme, oregano, marjoram, rosemary and savoury combine for aromatic addition to pizzas, stews, grilled foods and baked vegetables.

Herb Vinegars

Popular in earlier times when seasonings were limited, flavourful herb vinegars are being rediscovered by modern cooks. Useful for varying simple oil and vinegar salad dressings, herb vinegars can add depth to marinades, stews and sauces. The classic vinegar herb is tarragon, but dill, basil, thyme and rosemary are all suitable, on their own or in combinations with a bruised clove of garlic.

---

packed teacupful of chopped herbs
³/₄ pt /425ml /scant 2 cups white wine vinegar

Place herbs in a sealable jar. Heat vinegar to just below boiling point, removing from heat before bubbles start to surface; pour over herbs in jar. Seal tightly and keep for two weeks, shaking occasionally. Strain vinegar and transfer to clean bottle. For decorative touch, add sprig of herb used before sealing bottle.

Herb Oils

A resurgence of Mediterranean cooking has popularized olive oil and herb-flavoured varieties of this "butter of the South". Delicious herb-scented oil flavours pasta and grilled foods as well as salad dressings and looks too pretty to be shut in a cupboard.

---

good quality olive oil
one or more herbs: basil, chives, bay, garlic, sage rosemary, thyme
optional additions: chilli peppers; red, green or
black peppercorns; strips of lemon peel

Wash and dry the herbs to be used and slightly bruise the leaves. Pour over the oil and leave in a dark place for two weeks. Taste, and if stronger flavour is desired, add more herbs and leave for a further week. Strain oil and decant into clean bottles, decorating with fresh sprigs of the herbs used..

Mustard and Dill Mayonnaise

This slightly sweet-and-sharp sauce complements poached salmon as well as other cold seafood and makes an excellent dressing for potato and cooked vegetable salads. It is best made a little in advance so that flavours can blend.

---

2 tbsp French mustard
2 tbsp tarragon vinegar
2 tsp caster sugar
$^1/_2$ tsp salt
pinch of white pepper
2 egg yolks
$^1/_4$ pt /150ml /scant $^2/_3$ cup olive or salad oil
3 tbsp chopped fresh dill
warm water

Start with all ingredients at room temperature. Beat together the mustard, vinegar, sugar, salt, pepper and egg yolks. Beat in oil drop by drop, increasing flow when about one-third of the oil has been incorporated. Stir in dill, correct seasoning if necessary and thin to desired consistency with a little warm water if wished. Cover and keep in a cool place.

Pesto

Richly scented basil combines with garlic, pine kernels and cheese in one of the classic Mediterranean sauces for pasta. In southern France the same mixture is called *pistou* and is stirred into home-made vegetable soup. It is also delicious as a dip for raw vegetables or sauce for cold sliced lamb.

1 packed cupful fresh basil leaves	*4 tbsp freshly grated Parmesan cheese*
1 clove garlic, peeled	*6–8 tbsp olive oil*
2 tbsp pine kernels	*salt*

Put basil, garlic, pine kernels and cheese into a blender with a spoonful of oil. Process briefly into a paste. Continue to process while slowly trickly in remaining oil to make a creamy sauce. Season to taste with salt.

Rosemary Potatoes

Wonderfully fragrant, crispy potatoes are the soul of simplicity, effortlessly cooked alongside roast chicken or other oven-baked meals.

3 tbsp chopped fresh rosemary	*4 baking potatoes*
2 tbsp coarse sea salt	*cooking oil*

Mix rosemary and sea salt together. Halve the potatoes lengthwise and brush skin and cut surfaces generously with oil. Dip cut surface

of each potato into the rosemary-salt mixture and place cut side down on baking tray. Bake in oven pre-heated to gas mark 5, 375°C, 190°C until potato is done through and cut side is golden brown.

Parsley Tomatoes

Nothing could be simpler than this salad of juicy sun-ripened tomatoes. It is one of the few fresh salads that benefits from being dressed well before serving.

5–6 large ripe tomatoes
large handful of parsley, finely chopped
small bunch of chives, chopped
3 tbsp olive oil
2 tbsp white wine vinegar
1 tsp sugar
1/2 tsp salt
black pepper

Slice tomatoes thickly and layer them into a shallow dish with the chopped parsley and chives. Combine the remaining ingredients to make dressing and pour over tomatoes. Leave in a cool place for an hour or two. Serve at room temperature.

Bruschetta

This Mediterranean olive pickers' snack originated from the custom of tasting the newly pressed oil on chunks of bread. Topped with ripe tomatoes or even bits of cheese and ham, it makes a tasty light meal or first course.

thickly sliced country bread	olive oil
clove of garlic, cut in half	selection of chopped fresh herbs:
sliced tomatoes	marjoram, parsley,
salt, pepper	oregano, chives, thyme

Toast the bread on both sides. Rub the cut side of the garlic over toast, as lightly or lavishly as wished. Top with sliced tomatoes, sprinkle with salt and pepper and drizzle with olive oil. Put under hot grill for a minute, just until tomato starts to colour. Sprinkle thickly with chopped herbs and serve immediately.

Italian-Style Stuffed Mushrooms

Mediterranean herbs and anchovies in mushroom caps make an excellent starter or accompaniment for plain grilled meat, fish or pasta.

12 large open mushrooms
olive oil
2 oz /50g /1 cup fresh breadcrumbs
3 tbsp finely chopped onion
1 clove garlic, finely chopped

2 ripe tomatoes, peeled and chopped
6 anchovy fillets, drained and chopped
3 tbsp finely chopped parsley
1 tbsp fresh oregano leaves, chopped
salt, pepper

Clean mushrooms and carefully remove stalks. Chop stalks, heat a little olive oil in a frying pan and lightly sauté the stalks with breadcrumbs, onion and garlic. Remove from heat, stir in remaining ingredients and season to taste with salt and pepper.

Heap stuffing into mushroom caps and place in greased baking dish. Drizzle a little olive oil over and bake in oven pre-heated to gas mark 6, 400°F, 200°C for about 20 minutes.

Country Herb and Pork Pâté

This rough-textured home-made pâté is flecked with fresh herbs, perfect for serving with toast or crusty bread.

---

8 oz/225g lean pork pieces	large handful finely chopped herbs:
8 oz/225g pork belly, diced	parsley, marjoram, thyme, sage
4 oz/100g smoked bacon, diced	2 tbsp lemon juice
2 oz/50g/1 cup breadcrumbs	2 tbsp dry sherry
1 onion, chopped	1 egg, beaten
1–2 cloves garlic, crushed	salt, pepper

(serves 8)

Put pork and bacon through a mincer with the breadcrumbs, onion, garlic and herbs. Stir well to blend and add lemon juice, sherry and egg. Season with salt and pepper, turn into a well-greased 1½ pint/850ml/4 cups ovenproof dish and cover. Stand dish in a baking tin and fill halfway up with water. Bake in oven pre-heated to gas mark 4, 350°F, 180°C for 1½ hours. Cool pâté in the dish with a weighted plate on top. Chill overnight before turning out and serving.

Marinated Goat's Cheese

Herb-sprigged little rounds of cheese in golden oil make lovely gifts, especially at Easter, which marks the beginning of the season for fresh goat's cheese. If goat's cheese is crumbly, beat in small amounts of cream until it is easier to handle. The same recipe works well for other types of fresh cream cheese.

---

goat's cheese, creamy style
garlic cloves, peeled
small red chilli peppers
bay leaves
rosemary leaves
fresh thyme sprigs
green, rose and black peppercorns
olive oil

Form cheese into walnut-size balls and put lightly into jars. For each jar, put in one or two cloves of garlic, one or two chilli peppers, one bay leaf and a few rosemary leaves, a couple of thyme sprigs and about a heaped teaspoonful of peppercorns. Cover with oil, seal jars and store in a refrigerator or cool place for two weeks before using.

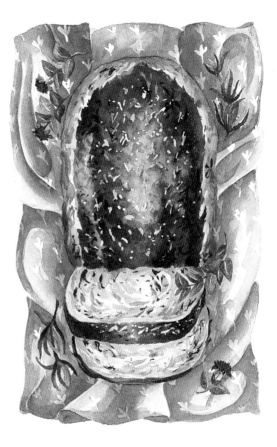

Country-Style Herb Bread

The new instant or "easy blend" yeast makes home baking a breeze even for novice cooks. Invent your own variations using different herbs, nuts, olives and seasonings. Strong flour has a high gluten content that gives best results in yeast baking.

---

1 lb /450g /4 cups strong flour
4½ oz/125g /1 cup wholemeal flour
2 tsp salt
2 tbsp olive oil
1 pkt (¼ oz/7g) instant dried yeast
15 fl oz/425ml/1 scant pint warm water
large handful freshly chopped herbs: thyme,
rosemary, marjoram, oregano, etc.
sea salt crystals, fresh herb sprigs to garnish

Combine flours with salt and olive oil, stir in yeast and add enough water to make soft dough. Turn onto a floured board and knead in chopped herbs. Continue kneading for 8–10 minutes, until dough is smooth and elastic. Shape dough into oval loaf and place on oiled baking tray. Sprinkle with salt crystals and sprigs of herbs if using. Cover loosely with a polythene bag and leave in a warm place to rise until doubled, 1½–2 hours. Bake about 25 minutes in oven pre-heated to gas mark 8, 450°F, 230°C.

Rosemary Corn Muffins

Fragrant, grainy-textured muffins are quick to make. Serve hot with melted butter for brunch or a simple supper of scrambled eggs. Make tiny ones for a party, split and topped with baked ham, smoked chicken or turkey.

---

9 oz/250g/2 cups yellow cornmeal
5 oz/150g/1 cup plain flour
4 heaped tsp baking powder
1 tsp salt
2 tbsp sugar
2 oz/50g/¼ cup melted butter
2 eggs, beaten
scant ½ pt/280ml/1 cup milk
2 tbsp finely chopped rosemary

Combine dry ingredients with melted butter, beat in eggs and just enough milk to make a soft dropping batter. Stir in rosemary and spoon into well-greased muffin tins, filling half full. Bake until golden brown, 15–20 minutes, in oven pre-heated to gas mark 6, 400°F, 200°C.

Garlic Soup

A whole head of garlic may sound excessive, but this typical French country soup demonstrates the taming influence of gentle cooking. The pungent herb is reduced to savoury sweetness, and acquires meal status when the resulting soup is ladled over a poached egg and croutons.

---

2 medium onions, sliced
1 head of garlic, sliced finely
1 tbsp olive oil
2 tbsp flour
2¹/₂ pt/1.5 ltr/6 cups chicken stock
2–3 tsp lemon juice
salt, pepper
2 eggs, beaten

Sweat the onions and garlic with the oil in a large heavy-bottomed pan over low heat, making sure they soften without colouring. Stir in the flour, cook for a further minute, then pour in the chicken stock. Bring to the boil, reduce heat and simmer for 25 minutes. Strain the soup, pressing through as much purée as possible. Season to taste with the lemon juice, salt and pepper. Beat a small amount of warm soup into the eggs, then blend the egg mixture into the soup and reheat without boiling. Serve with crusty bread or croutons.

Thai Lemon and Coriander Soup

Exotic, yet quick and easy to make, this is the sort of food that makes a reputation for a brilliant cook. Warming in winter and refreshing in summer, this soup is a perfect starter for an Eastern-style meal of curry, kebabs or *tandoori*.

---

1 ½ pt/850ml/4 cups chicken stock
2 tbsp hot curry paste
1 chicken breast fillet, shredded
1–2 tbsp lemon juice
1 small red chilli pepper, de-seeded and sliced finely
small bunch fresh coriander leaves, chopped

Put stock and curry paste in a pan over medium heat and stir to dissolve. Bring just to boil, add chicken breast and lemon juice, reduce heat and simmer gently for about 8 minutes, until chicken is done. Taste and correct seasoning if necessary. Serve hot with the chilli pepper and coriander stirred through.

Cold Cucumber and Dill Soup

Refreshing and delicious no-cook soup is easy to make and special enough for the most formal of parties.

I large cucumber
$^1\!/_2$ clove garlic, crushed
1 pt//570ml/2$^1\!/_4$ cups natural yogurt
$^1\!/_2$ pt/280ml/1 generous cup light chicken stock
2 tbsp dill, finely chopped
salt
4 tbsp cream
sprigs of dill and mint leaves to garnish

Peel cucumber, de-seed and grate or chop very finely. Put half the cucumber into food processor with garlic, yogurt and stock and blend until smooth. Stir in remaining cucumber and dill. Taste and add salt if needed. Chill for several hours to allow flavours to blend. Serve with a swirl of cream on each portion, garnished with dill sprigs and mint leaves.

Potato, Dill and Egg Salad

A light but tasty potato salad dressed while warm and enhanced with fresh herbs is a perfect accompaniment for cold or grilled meat or barbecues.

I lb/450g new potatoes	4 tbsp celery tops, finely chopped
6 tbsp olive oi	2 tbsp chopped dill

2 tbsp white wine vinegar	2 tbsp chopped chives
1 tsp wholegrain mustard	4 hardboiled eggs
pinch of sugar	bunch of watercress
salt, pepper	

Wash and cook the potatoes in their skins. While they are cooking, mix together the olive oil, vinegar, mustard, sugar, salt and pepper to taste. Quickly halve the cooked potatoes (or slice if they are large) and pour dressing over while they are still hot. Allow to cool a little and stir in celery, dill and chives. Cut eggs into eighths and toss lightly through salad. Serve in shallow dish wreathed with watercress.

Greek Country Salad

Sunny Mediterranean vegetables combine with the herbs that grow wild on Greek hillsides. If Greek-style feta is not available, substitute *chèvre* or goat cheese.

1 lb/450g tomatoes, sliced	1 tbsp torn oregano leaves
1 green pepper, shredded	1 tsp thyme leaves
1 large onion, thinly sliced	1/2 lemon
1/2 cucumber, peeled and sliced	4 tbsp olive oil
4 oz/110g feta cheese, diced	salt, pepper
handful of black olives	

Arrange vegetables attractively in shallow dish. Strew with the cheese, olives, oregano and thyme. Squeeze lemon juice over and drizzle with olive oil. Season with salt and pepper to taste.

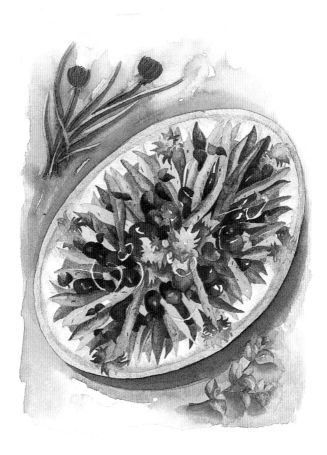

Herb and Bean Salad

Delicious and full of protein, this attractive salad can be made in advance and travels well for picnics and outdoor entertaining. The selection of herbs can be varied to suit the season, winter or summer.

---

8 oz/225g French beans, topped and tailed
1 clove garlic, crushed
1 tin (14½ oz/410g) red kidney beans, drained
5 tbsp olive oil
4 tbsp red wine vinegar
2 tsp sugar
1 tsp salt
½ cup finely chopped mixed herbs: parsley,
marjoram, thyme, tarragon, chives
1 small onion, thinly sliced

Cook the French beans with the garlic until tender in a little boiling water. Drain and combine while hot with the remaining ingredients except onion. Mix thoroughly, cover and allow flavours to blend for at least an hour. Serve garnished with the sliced onion rings.

Herb and Cheese Omelette

This is a classic meal-in-a-minute recipe, made tasty with fresh green herbs. For picnics or packed lunches, pack the cooked omelette into a hollowed-out crusty loaf and cut into thick slices.

---

8 large eggs
1 tbsp chopped fresh chives
1 tbsp chopped fresh tarragon
1 tbsp chopped fresh parsley
4 tbsp freshly grated Parmesan or other hard cheese
salt, pepper
1 tbsp oil or butter

Beat eggs lightly in a bowl and stir in chopped herbs, cheese, salt and pepper. Heat oil or butter in a frying pan, pour in egg mixture and cook without stirring, occasionally loosening edges and allowing loose mixture to run underneath. When omelette bottom is firm and top is no longer runny, slice it onto plate, invert pan over it, reverse and return to heat to brown underneath. Serve cut into quarters.

Courgette-Dill Pasta

Courgettes combine with pasta and herbs in a healthy meatless dish that is especially attractive when both yellow and green varieties of the vegetable are available.

---

14 oz/400g spaghetti or other pasta
2 tbsp olive oil
4–5 courgettes, sliced
1 small onion, chopped
3 tbsp chopped fresh dill
4 tbsp sour cream
salt, pepper
grated cheese

Cook spaghetti or other pasta according to directions on packet. Meanwhile, heat oil in a large frying pan and gently stir-fry courgettes and onions until soft and slightly coloured. Stir in fresh dill and sour cream and heat until warm. When pasta is cooked, drain and combine with courgette mixture. Serve sprinkled with grated cheese.

Seafood and Herb Salad

A light dish suitable for a first course, buffet dish or summer main course, this seafood combination improves when made a little in advance. Use whatever white fish is in good supply and vary by adding bits of smoked fish or shellfish if wished.

1 lb/450g firm white fish fillets (hake, halibut, haddock, monkfish)	5 tbsp olive oil
	4 tbsp lemon juice
	1 tbsp chopped parsley
lemon slices	1 tbsp chopped fresh fennel
bay leaf	salt, pepper
4 oz/110g cooked peeled prawns	snipped chives
4 spring onions, shredded	fennel sprigs

Poach fish fillets in a little water with lemon slices and bay leaf. Drain, cool and break into large flakes, removing any skin or bones. Place in a large bowl with prawns and spring onions. Combine olive oil, lemon juice, parsley and fennel with salt and pepper to taste, pour over seafood and toss lightly to mix. Garnish with chives and fennel sprigs.

Summer Chicken

A recipe for midsummer, when rampant mint is at its best for using in great handfuls. The spicy Middle Eastern marinade subtly quells the strength of the mint.

chicken portions for 4	juice of 1 lemon
2 cloves garlic	2 tbsp good cooking oil
1 tsp coriander seed	6 tbsp natural yogurt
3 tsp cumin seed	salt
$\frac{1}{2}$ tsp ground cinnamon	large handful of fresh mint,
1 tsp ground turmeric	coarsely chopped

Skin the chicken portions and slash thick parts. Grind or blend together the garlic, coriander and cumin seeds, then combine with other ingredients except mint. Pour the spice mixture over chicken in a bowl and leave to marinate for at least an hour. When ready to cook, lay mint in a greased ovenproof dish and top with chicken portions and the marinade. Cover and bake in oven pre-heated to gas mark 4, 350°F, 180°C until chicken is cooked through. Remove chicken to warm serving dish, strain cooking juices and reduce quickly over heat. Pour resulting sauce over and garnish with fresh sprigs of mint.

Herb-Roasted Chicken

A certain amount of care is required to work herb-rich butter under the skin of plump roasting fowl, but the deliciously moist and flavourful result is worth the effort.

1 large roasting chicken	2 tsp fresh chopped marjoram
2 oz/50g/4 tbsp butter	1 tsp fresh chopped rosemary
1 tbsp fresh chopped tarragon	1 tsp grated lemon rind
2 tsp fresh chopped thyme	salt, pepper

Clean the chicken inside and out and, working from the neck flap, carefully work fingers between the skin and flesh to loosen skin over the breast and tops of the legs. Work the butter to a soft paste with the chopped herbs and lemon rind. Divide into walnut-size pieces and place under the skin, massaging the outer surface to spread butter more or less evenly over breast and legs. Spread a little butter on top of skin, sprinkle with salt and pepper and roast in oven pre-heated to gas mark 6, 400°F, 200°C for about 15 minutes to the pound, or until juices run clear.

Chicken with Tarragon

There are many versions of the classic French *poulet à l'estragon* simply because chicken and tarragon go so well together. Make this delicious dish extra special by using chicken breast fillets instead of the whole bird.

1 tbsp butter	4 large sprigs fresh tarragon
1 large roasting chicken, jointed	salt, pepper
1/2 pt/225ml/1 1/4 cups white wine	1/4 pt/150ml/2/3 cup cream
1/2 pt/225ml/1 1/4 cups water	8–10 fresh tarragon leaves

Heat butter in a heavy-bottomed pan and brown chicken pieces. Pour in wine and water, add tarragon, salt and pepper and bring to the boil. Cover tightly, reduce heat and simmer for about 45 minutes or until chicken is cooked through. Remove chicken pieces to serving dish and keep warm. Strain cooking juices and reduce quickly to about 1/4 pt/150ml/2/3 cup. Add cream and simmer gently until sauce is slightly thickened; taste and correct seasoning. Pour sauce over chicken in serving dish and scatter with tarragon leaves.

Fresh Herb Sausages

Tasty home-made sausages without the cereals and fillers of commercial products are surprisingly easy to make, even for novice cooks. This recipe can also be adapted to make sausages of venison or other meats.

---

12 oz/340g lean pork meat
6 oz/170g pork back fat
1 1/2 tsp salt
1/2 tsp or more coarsely ground black pepper
2 tbsp finely chopped parsley
2 tsp chopped fresh sage
2 tsp chopped thyme leaves
pinch of ground allspice
pinch of ground mace
clove of garlic, crushed (optional)
flour or fine breadcrumbs

Put all the ingredients except flour or breadcrumbs through a mincer once, or twice if a finer texture is preferred. When ready to cook, form into patties or sausage shapes using flour or breadcrumbs to prevent sticking. Cook by pan frying or grilling.

Jambon Persillé

This classic dish of cold ham set in savoury green jelly is an Easter tradition in France and makes a striking buffet centrepiece.

4–5 lb/2kg piece of boneless ham
1 tsp whole black peppercorns
1 stalk celery
1 bouquet garni (p. 11)
8 fl oz/225ml/1 cup white wine
lemon juice
5 tsp powdered gelatin
2 packed cups finely chopped parsley

Soak the ham overnight if necessary, then place in a pot with water to cover and add the peppercorns, celery and *bouquet garni*. Simmer ham until cooked thoroughly.

Remove ham, cool and dice roughly into $^3/_4$ inch/2cm pieces, removing all fat. Pack loosely into bowl or dish to be used as a mould. De-fat stock, strain and heat with white wine, reducing a little. Add lemon juice and correct seasoning if necessary. Soften gelatin in a little cold water, then add to 2 pints/1 litre of hot stock and stir until completely dissolved. Allow to cool slightly and stir in chopped parsley. Pour stock mixture over the chopped ham in dish and leave to set overnight in a cool place. When ready to use, turn out on a platter and serve in slices.

Sage and Onion Stuffed Pork Chops

Sage and onion have been successful culinary partners since Roman times, an especially happy combination for pork as well as duck and chicken.

---

4 thick-cut pork chops, boneless
2 tbsp butter or oil
1 onion, chopped
2 oz/50g/1 cup fresh breadcrumbs
10–12 fresh sage leaves, chopped
salt, pepper
4 fl oz/110ml/¹/₂ cup wine or stock

Cut a slit lengthwise into the chops to form a pocket for stuffing. Heat butter in a frying pan and cook onion until just soft. Add breadcrumbs, sage, salt and pepper and stir briefly over heat until breadcrumbs are slightly toasted. When mixture is cooled, pack into the pork chops and secure with a small skewer or cocktail stick. Brown the stuffed chops quickly on both sides, pour in wine or stock, cover tightly and lower heat. Simmer chops until cooked through, adding a little water if necessary. Serve with cooking juices spooned over.

Lamb Chops with Mint and Lemon Sauce

A lemony tang brings fresh flavour to this updated version of traditional mint sauce. It can also be brushed on to give a final glaze to roast leg of lamb.

---

lamb chops for 4 persons
2 tbsp olive oil
2 tsp chopped fresh rosemary
4 oz/110ml/¹/₂ cup redcurrant jelly
1 tbsp sugar
4 tbsp lemon juice
3 tbsp water
4 tbsp chopped fresh mint leaves
salt, pepper

Toss the lamb chops in oil and rosemary and marinate in refrigerator for an hour or two. Make sauce by melting redcurrant jelly and sugar with lemon juice and water in a small pan. When jelly is completely dissolved, remove from heat and stir in mint leaves.

Season lamb chops with salt and pepper and grill on both sides. When nearly done, brush with mint sauce and return to grill until nicely glazed. Serve with extra mint sauce to spoon over.

Leg of Lamb in a Herb Crust

Succulent roast lamb rises to aromatic heights with a finishing coat of golden breadcrumbs and herbs. This recipe works equally well with a shoulder or rack of lamb or even individual lamb chops finished under the grill.

---

1 leg of lamb
5 tbsp fresh breadcrumbs
2 tbsp chopped parsley
1 tbsp chopped mint
2 tsp chopped rosemary
1 clove garlic, finely chopped
2 tbsp lemon juice
2 tsp sugar
salt, pepper

Place prepared lamb in oven pre-heated to gas mark 7, 425°F, 220°C. Reduce heat to gas mark 4, 350°F, 180°C and cook for 18–25 minutes per pound, depending on doneness desired. Combine remaining ingredients to make a paste, adding a little water if necessary. Thirty minutes before lamb is done, remove from oven and spread with herb mixture. Spoon over a little of the pan juices and return to oven to finish cooking.

Index